Rahab's Red Rope

Storyline **Sue A. Smith**
Illustrations **Steven Butler**

Rahab looked out from her house that was tall, up near the top of the Jericho wall.

Israel's army was camped round about,
ready to march and ready to shout!

Strangers arrived at her home one night,
two men who spoke of the upcoming fight.

They talked of their God, and she wished to hear more, when suddenly there was a knock at her door!

The two men were spies looking over the town.
They must get out now without being found!

"Go up on my roof! Lie flat on the floor. I'll hide
you with flax 'til you're safe once more."

Jericho's king hoped to catch the two men.
He shut the big gates so they had to stay in.

But Rahab had trust, and Rahab had hope.
Out of her window she hung a strong rope.

"Climb down," said Rahab, "down Jericho's wall.
Your God is a great God, he won't let you fall."

"But make me a promise," said Rahab the kind.
"I'm saving your lives now, so won't you save mine?"

The spies said to Rahab, "God cares for you, too.
Your family we'll save, but this you must do..."

"Our army will know of your faith and your hope,
if out of this window you hang a red rope."

Down went the spies from her roof to the ground,
back to the army with what they had found.

And Rahab had faith, and Rahab had hope.
Out of her window she hung the red rope.

So Israel marched, and the walls tumbled down,
but Rahab's family was kept safe and sound.